Retrieving and managing email

with POP3 and C#

from the author of
OstroSoft POP3 Component

IGOR OSTROVSKY

Copyright © 2014 Igor Ostrovsky

All rights reserved.

ISBN: 1503318451
ISBN-13: 978-1503318458

CONTENTS

	Preface	7
1	Quick look at POP3	9
2	Sample POP3 Session	11
3	Designing POP3 client	15
4	General declarations	18
5	GUI and Session state	19
6	Connecting to POP3 server	21
7	Handling a secure connection	25
8	Reading server responses	28
9	Sending POP3 commands	31
10	Server status and QUIT command	32
11	Authentication (commands USER and PASS)	35
12	Retrieving mailbox stats (STAT command)	37
13	Getting message list (LIST command)	38
14	Finalizing btnConnect_Click() method	39
15	Session reset (RSET command)	41

16	Deleting a message (DELE command)	42
17	Email message format	43
18	Retrieving messages (RETR and TOP commands)	46
19	frmMessage	48
20	ParsePart() method	50
21	LoadHeaders() method	52
22	DecodeString() method	54
23	Decoding functions (Base64 and Quoted-Printable)	56
24	LoadBody() method	58
25	Saving the message	60
26	Running the application	61
	Links and references	66

Preface

Email is one of the most popular parts of the Internet. One of the oldest too.

Older than Google and Facebook.
Older than the Web.
Older than dinosaurs (not sure about this one, though).

The idea behind email is really simple:
- one person, sender, creates a message, then sends it
- another person, recipient, retrieves the message and reads it (not always the case).

Early email systems existed even before the Internet and were proprietary - there was no interoperability between them.

The situation changed in early 70-s, when ARPA started to standardize cross-networks communications.
The result is well-known and quite popular - the Internet.
As a part of standardization, common protocols were created for sending and retrieving email.

Time passed, email standards kept growing - covering authentication, message format, relay and storage, encoding, attachments, and many other important aspects.
The full list of these beautifully boring yet absolutely necessary standards is available at Internet Mail Consortium web page (http://web.archive.org/web/20120403094950/http://www.imc.org/rfcs.html).
And it's a huge list. Amount of information it contains is overwhelming. Luckily, we don't have to read it all.

Oversimplified breakdown of standards goes like this:
- SMTP is used to send emails
- POP3 and IMAP are used to retrieve emails from mailserver
- RFC5322 covers message format
- MIME takes care of attachments

This book concentrates on POP3 - the most popular protocol to retrieve and manage email messages.

Why write a book on POP3

When it comes to programming, it appears there is much less attention devoted to retrieving email than to sending it.

For example, Microsoft has a very mature and functionally rich software libraries for sending email via SMTP:
- system.net.mail for .NET
- CDO for COM

No such luck with POP3.
There is nothing from Microsoft. Few POP3 libraries are available from 3rd parties.

There are countless books covering all aspects of SMTP - from the basics to most advanced concepts.
Yet very few books are written about POP3. And practically all of them tend to be solid references, paying the most attention to standards and protocols, but very little - to practical programming.

This book will help you build POP3 client application in C# while emphasizing on programming aspects and minimizing an information overload from learning the email standards.

If you are on a tight schedule or don't want to get into programming details, simply download a compiled library at
http://www.ostrosoft.com/ospop3.aspx

Retrieving and managing email with POP3 and C#

1. Quick look at POP3

Terminology

POP3 is an Internet standard, defining the way to retrieve messages from mailserver and manage mailboxes.

POP3 stands for Post Office Protocol version 3 and was first introduced in 1996.

Mailserver is a software accepting email messages from senders, relaying them to destination mailservers and storing incoming email into recipients' mailboxes

Email address uniquely identifies locations of message sender and recipient.
If recipient's address is invalid, the message doesn't get delivered. Based on mailserver settings, a message to invalid recipient may get redirected to administrative "catch-all" mailbox, bounced back to a sender with a "failed delivery" notification or simply ignored.

Mailbox is a storage area in mailserver dedicated to a particular email address. Owner of the mailbox logs in to his mailserver to retrieve and manage his messages.

POP3 is a **client-server protocol**.
POP3 client and mailserver are taking turns to communicate with each other: - client sends a request with a command understood by POP3 server - server returns a response with the result of the command preceded by a status of its execution

POP3 is **text-based** - it supports only ASCII characters.

All non-ASCII characters are encoded as plain text, either in Base64 or in Quoted-Printable encodings (for example, that's how binary attachments are emailed).

POP3 is **session-based**.

Client establishes a connection to a mailserver, authenticates, then retrieves or deletes messages in a mailbox. Session has to be gracefully closed by QUIT command issued by client, otherwise all changes made during it will be lost.

Below is the list of most common POP3 commands grouped by functionality.

1. Authentication:
USER [user-name]
followed by **PASS [password]**
2. Message retrieval and management:
LIST - retrieve a list of messages
RETR [message-number] - retrieve a message
TOP [message-number] [number-of-lines] - retrieve message headers and top lines of message body
DELE [message-number] - delete a message
3. Mailbox status and info:
STAT - show mailbox statistics (number of messages and their total size)
RSET - reset the session (undeletes deleted messages)
QUIT - close the session

2. Sample POP3 Session

The easiest way to understand how POP3 works is to run a POP3 session in telnet client (for testing Gmail and other services requiring secure connection you will need a telnet client supporting SSL).

Open a telnet client of your choice and connect to your mailserver. You can use either server name or IP address. POP3 is typically running on port 110.

```
> telnet mail.testserver.test 110
```

Upon successful connection mailserver will respond with a status string:

```
+OK <15237.1409568095@mail.testserver.test>
```

If connection fails, then it was probably caused by one of the following:
- mailserver name or IP address is invalid
- POP3 is running on a non-standard port (check your email settings to find the right one)
- connection is blocked by your firewall or antivirus

* If you received -ERR status response, then you are not allowed to access specified mailserver (your IP is either blacklisted or not in a whitelist) or mailserver is currently down or not accepting new connections.

Now it's time to authenticate:

```
USER test
+OK
PASS mypassword
+OK
```

* -ERR status response means that credentials supplied by you are not valid.

At this point POP3 session is established and we can start working with mailbox contents.

```
STAT
+OK 20 570723
```

Response to STAT command shows that mailbox contains 20 messages with a total size 570723 bytes.

Let's get a breakdown by message:

```
LIST
+OK
1 8483
2 3717
3 4011
[... I skipped some messages to preserve space ...]
18 3150
19 3133
20 15312
.
```

Now we have a message size for each message in a mailbox.

Period at the end of the output means just that - the end of output.

Each POP3 command returning a multiline response ends with a period.

I want to view the last message in the mailbox:

```
RETR 20
+OK
Received: from unknown (HELO xssgktkzzfbmdh)
(109.68.237.12)
   by mail.testserver.test with ESMTP; 22 Jul 2014 12:55:49
-0000
X-Originating-IP: 109.68.237.12
Received-SPF: none (mail.testserver.test: domain at
ubno.com does not designate permitted sender hosts)
        identity=mailfrom; client-ip=109.68.237.12;
        envelope-from=<ociuufhdvlf@ubno.com>;
To: test
From: "Get-Viigarra N0w" <ociuufhdvlf@ubno.com>
Subject: Vigara Noow == 0.77$
Date: Fri, 2 Jan 1970 00:04:16 +0000
X-Priority: 3
X-MSMail-Priority: Normal
X-Mailer: IPB PHP Mailer
MIME-Version: 1.0
Content-Transfer-Encoding: 8bit
Content-Type: text/html; charset="UTF-8"
Message-ID: <19700102000416.82813118cw109@xssgktkzzfbmdh>

<!DOCTYPE HTML PUBLIC "-//W3C//DTD HTML 4.01
Transitional//EN">
<html><head>
   <meta content="text/html; charset=utf-8" http-
equiv="Content-Type">
   <title>jwhnmmvwqqqffbnqcmuym</title>
   <style type="text/css">
        a:hover  text-decoration: none !important;
        .header p  serif; margin: 0; padding: 0; line-
height: 11px; letter-spacing: 2px
[… part of the message body is not shown to preserve space
…]
           <tr>
              <td
 style="margin: 0pt; padding: 15px 0pt 10px; font-size:
11px; font-family: Georgia,serif;" align="center"
bgcolor="#698291" valign="top">
              <span style="background-color: #698291">Have a
nice day!</span></td>
           </tr>
        </tbody>
      </table>
<!-- footer--> </td>
     </tr>
   </tbody>
</table>
</body></html>
.
```

Wow, look at this beauty - it's one of them viagra emails!

Unfortunate sign of the times - the very first email we tried to read is spam. And it's quite unreadable (we will deal with that "unreadable" thingy later, when we get to message parsing).

So, what's the first reaction to a message like this? Of course we want to reply!

Nah, just kidding. This stuff should be deleted ASAP:

```
DELE 20
+OK
```

That's it. Gone!

Gone? Remember that part about gracefully closing the connection?

If we just kill the telnet window now, the next time we connect to a mailserver our favorite message number 20 will still be there.

We need to give mailserver a chance to apply and save changes we made.

Here. Much better:

```
QUIT
+OK
```

And that concludes our POP3 session.

Technically, we could keep reading email from a telnet client. And we used to, before binary attachments and HTML parts were introduced.

These days we need to dig deeper if we want to make sense of all message content.

But enough talking - let's code!

3. Designing POP3 client

Open Visual Studio, create new Windows Forms Application in C#, name it **POP3_Client**.
* The user interface can be anything - WPF, ASP.NET, even command-line utility, but for simplicity sake we'll use good old Windows Forms.

By default, Visual Studio creates a form called Form1. Rename it to **frmSession**.

This will be our main form, containing connection-related fields and displaying mailbox data - size, number of messages, list of messages and buttons to manage them.

Add GroupBox control to the form, name it **gbConnectionSettings**.

Add the following TextBox controls to Session GroupBox: **txtServer**, **txtPort**, **txtUsername** and **txtPassword** with corresponding labels.

Add CheckBox control named **chkUseSecureConnection**.

```
Connection settings
    Server  [           ]       Username  [           ]
    Port    [           ]       Password  [           ]
            [ ] Use secure connection
```

This section holds connection and authentication settings.

Below **gbConnectionSettings** groupbox add Button control named **btnConnect**.

The button will serve dual purpose: connect to mailserver when there is no POP3 session in progress and quit the established POP3 session.

Add another GroupBox control to the form, name it **gbMailboxContents**.

Add the following Button controls to it: **btnResetSession, btnRefreshMsgList, btnViewMessage, btnViewHeaders** and **btnDeleteMessage**.

Add the following TextBox controls: **txtMailboxSize** and **txtMessageCount** with corresponding labels.

Add ListView control **lvwMessages** with 2 columns (ID, Size).

Completed groupbox should look like this:

Add a multi-line TextBox control to the form, name it **txtStatus**.
And that completes Session form layout.

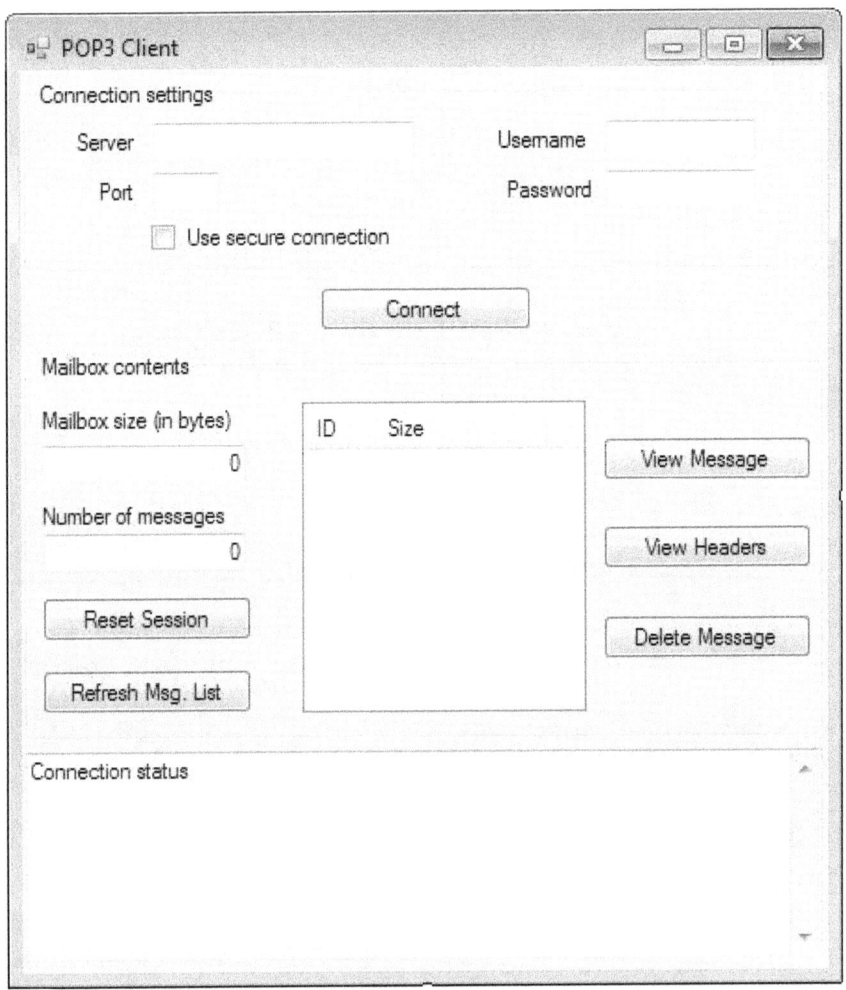

Looks good.
Let's put some code behind it.

4. General declarations

Add the following to the standard WinForm headers:

```
using System.Net.Security;
using System.Net.Sockets;
using System.Security.Cryptography.X509Certificates;
```

We need these for connecting to POP3 server (some of them are for secure connections required by Gmail, Yahoo Mail and many other providers).

Declare the following variables:

```
private TcpClient _client;
private NetworkStream _networkStream;
private SslStream _sslStream;

private string _command = "";
private string _response = "";
private enum State { Closed = 0, Connecting, Connected,
Authenticating, Authenticated, Closing };
```

`_client` is an abstraction of Windows socket - object providing connectivity to a remote host (POP3 server in our case).
`_networkStream` will be used for reading data from `_client`, `_sslStream` will be used for reading data from `_client` over secure connection (if necessary).
`_command` holds POP3 commands issued by client.
`_response` will contain mailserver responses.
`State` enumeration defines the states of POP3 session.

5. GUI and Session state

There was a reason we put our form controls in group boxes - it's easier to manage their **Enabled** state.

For example, when there is no POP3 session in progress (connection is closed) connection properties should be enabled, but mailbox content controls should be disabled.

When session is established and the user is authenticated, then mailbox content is available, but connection properties aren't.

Otherwise, in intermediate states, pretty much everything should be disabled.

To handle it we will use the following method:

```
private void SetUI(State _state)
{
    txtStatus.Text += "\r\n# " + _state.ToString();
    switch (_state)
    {
        case State.Closed:
            gbConnectionSettings.Enabled = true;
            gbMailboxContents.Enabled = false;
            btnConnect.Enabled = true;
            btnConnect.Text = "Connect";
            break;
        case State.Authenticated:
            gbConnectionSettings.Enabled = false;
            gbMailboxContents.Enabled = true;
            btnConnect.Enabled = true;
```

```
                btnConnect.Text = "Quit";
                break;
            default:
                btnConnect.Enabled = false;
                gbConnectionSettings.Enabled = false;
                gbMailboxContents.Enabled = false;
                break;
        }
    }
```

The method will also take care of updating the status textbox and caption of connect button.

Double-click on **frmSession** - Visual Studio will generate code to handle form load event. Add a call to our SetUI method to set controls for closed connection:

```
private void frmSession_Load(object sender, EventArgs e)
{
    SetUI(State.Closed);
}
```

6. Connecting to POP3 server

Double-click on **btnConnect** in form designer.
It will generate a delegate in form designer module for button click event:

```
this.btnConnect.Click += new
System.EventHandler(this.btnConnect_Click);
```

and a method stub for the delegate in form class:

```
private void btnConnect_Click(object sender, EventArgs e)
{
}
```

Add the following code to `btnConnect_Click` method:

```
SetUI(State.Connecting);
try
{
    _client = new TcpClient(txtServer.Text,
Convert.ToInt32(txtPort.Text));
    SetUI(State.Connected);
}
catch (Exception ex)
{
    txtStatus.Text += "\r\n!" + ex.Message;
}
```

This section of code tries to establish a connection to the specified POP3 server and updates status textbox.

Before we go any further let's talk about what will be put into status textbox and how we are going to mark different status types. Essentially, there will be **4 types of status messages**:
- messages defining the current status of our TCP client (we will mark them with #)
- error messages (will be marked by !)
- commands we are sending to POP3 server (marked by <)
- POP3 server responses (marked by >)

Each status message will start on a new line (preceded with \r\n escape sequence).

It will make easier to understand (and debug, if necessary) the flow of our POP3 session.

As of now the complete code for frmSession should look like this:

```
using System;
using System.Net.Security;
using System.Net.Sockets;
using System.Security.Cryptography.X509Certificates;
using System.Windows.Forms;

namespace POP3_Client
{
    public partial class frmSession : Form
    {
        private TcpClient _client;
        private NetworkStream _networkStream;
        private SslStream _sslStream;

        private string _command = "";
        private string _response = "";
        private enum State { Closed = 0, Connecting, Connected, Authenticating, Authenticated, Closing };

        public frmSession()
        {
            InitializeComponent();
        }

        private void btnConnect_Click(object sender, EventArgs e)
        {
            SetUI(State.Connecting);
            try
            {
                _client = new TcpClient(txtServer.Text, Convert.ToInt32(txtPort.Text));
```

```csharp
            SetUI(State.Connected);
        }
        catch (Exception ex)
        {
            txtStatus.Text += "\r\n! " + ex.Message;
        }
    }

    private void SetUI(State _state)
    {
        txtStatus.Text += "\r\n# " + _state.ToString();
        switch (_state)
        {
            case State.Closed:
                gbConnectionSettings.Enabled = true;
                gbMailboxContents.Enabled = false;
                btnConnect.Enabled = true;
                btnConnect.Text = "Connect";
                break;
            case State.Authenticated:
                gbConnectionSettings.Enabled = false;
                gbMailboxContents.Enabled = true;
                btnConnect.Enabled = true;
                btnConnect.Text = "Quit";
                break;
            default:
                btnConnect.Enabled = false;
                gbConnectionSettings.Enabled = false;
                gbMailboxContents.Enabled = false;
                break;
        }
    }

    private void frmSession_Load(object sender, EventArgs e)
    {
        SetUI(State.Closed);
    }
}
}
```

Run the application and click Connect button - you'll get an error message in status textbox right away. Most likely, complaining about string format - and that's coming from failed `Convert.ToInt32(txtPort.Text)` call, since we didn't enter anything into **txtPort**.

To establish a connection we need to specify server (host name or IP address) and port (110, by default).

Once you do that and click **btnConnect** button, status textbox should display "Connected to " message.

If it doesn't - double-check your mail settings (server name and port number) to make sure you are connecting to a right place. Even if both are correct, connection may still fail because of your firewall settings. But let's hope for the best.

7. Handling a secure connection

Remember **chkUseSecureConnection** checkbox?

Well, it's there for a reason. These days more and more mailservers require secure connections from clients. Most of the industry heavyweights do - Gmail, Yahoo Mail, etc.

When we are connecting to those, make sure **chkUseSecureConnection** checkbox is checked. And let's add some code to handle it.

The following function binds client socket to a secure stream and authenticates if secure connection is selected. Otherwise it binds the client to a regular network stream.
If no errors were detected in process, function returns true.

```
private void SetConnectionType()
{
    if (chkUseSecureConnection.Checked)
    {
        try
        {
            _sslStream = new SslStream(_client.GetStream(), false, new RemoteCertificateValidationCallback (ValidateServerCertificate), null);
        }
        catch (Exception ex)
        {
            throw new Exception(ex.Message);
        }
```

```
        try
        {
_sslStream.AuthenticateAsClient(txtServer.Text);
        }
        catch
        {
            throw new Exception("Authentication failed - 
closing the connection");
        }
    }
    else
        _networkStream = _client.GetStream();
}
```

This subroutine processes certificates:

```
private bool ValidateServerCertificate(object sender,
X509Certificate certificate, X509Chain chain,
SslPolicyErrors sslPolicyErrors)
{
    if (sslPolicyErrors == SslPolicyErrors.None)
        return true;
    else
    {
        txtStatus.Text += "\r\n! Certificate error: " +
sslPolicyErrors;
        return false;
    }
}
```

And of course we need to call it from our btnConnect click event:

```
private void btnConnect_Click(object sender, EventArgs e)
{
    SetUI(State.Connecting);
    try
    {
        _client = new TcpClient(txtServer.Text,
Convert.ToInt32(txtPort.Text));
        SetUI(State.Connected);

        SetConnectionType();
    }
    catch (Exception ex)
    {
        txtStatus.Text += "\r\n! " + ex.Message;
    }
}
```

If you want to use POP3 client with Gmail, your server should be set to pop.gmail.com and port - to 995.

chkUseSecureConnection checkbox should be checked, of course.

8. Reading server responses

At this point we should be able to connect to POP3 server and bind POP3 client output to a corresponding stream (normal or secure).

The next logical step would be interacting with the server. For that I'm going to introduce few helper functions.

Function `Receive()` reads server response from TCP client buffer. Depending on a connection type it uses either a regular network stream or a secure one.

```
private string Receive()
{
    string reply = "";
    if (chkUseSecureConnection.Checked)
    {
        byte[] buffer = new byte[2048];
        StringBuilder messageData = new StringBuilder();
        int bytes = -1;
        do
        {
            bytes = _sslStream.Read(buffer, 0, buffer.Length);

            Decoder decoder = Encoding.UTF8.GetDecoder();
            char[] chars = new char[decoder.GetCharCount(buffer, 0, bytes)];
            decoder.GetChars(buffer, 0, bytes, chars, 0);

            messageData.Append(chars);
            if (IsComplete(messageData.ToString()))
                break;
```

```
        } while (bytes != 0);
        reply = messageData.ToString();
    }
    else
    {
        byte[] buffer = new byte[1024];
        int ret = _networkStream.Read(buffer, 0, buffer.Length);
        while (ret > 0)
        {
            reply += Encoding.UTF8.GetString(buffer, 0, ret);
            if (IsComplete(reply))
                break;
            ret = _networkStream.Read(buffer, 0, buffer.Length);
        }
    }

    txtStatus.Text += "\r\n> " + reply;
    return reply;
}
```

Since we are using `StringBuilder` we need to add a following declaration to the class headers:

```
using System.Text;
```

Boolean function `IsComplete(string reply)` indicates whether we should continue reading the buffer.

In case of an error it returns true right away, otherwise it checks for response terminator based on a command type.

POP3 commands like **LIST, UIDL, RETR, TOP** return multiline responses, terminated with `<CR><LF>.<CR><LF>` sequence. Otherwise, "hard" return signals the end of server response.

```
private bool IsComplete(string reply)
{
    if ((reply.ToUpper().StartsWith("-ERR")) && (reply.EndsWith("\r\n")))
        return true;

    switch (_command)
    {
        case "LIST":
        case "UIDL":
        case "RETR":
        case "TOP":
            if (reply.EndsWith("\r\n.\r\n"))
                return true;
            else
                return false;
        default:
            if (reply.EndsWith("\r\n"))
                return true;
            else
                return false;
    }
}
```

9. Sending POP3 commands

POP3 commands are simple and short. Sending them doesn't require much.

And it's reflected in Send function:

```
private void Send(string data)
{
    txtStatus.Text += "\r\n< " + data.TrimEnd();

    data += "\r\n";
    byte[] toSend = Encoding.UTF8.GetBytes(data);
    if (chkUseSecureConnection.Checked)
    {
        _sslStream.Write(toSend);
        _sslStream.Flush();
    }
    else
    {
        _networkStream.Write(toSend, 0, toSend.Length);
    }
}
```

10. Server status and QUIT command

POP3 server returns a status response as soon as client establishes connection.

The content of the response varies from implementation to implementation, but it always starts with +OK if connection was accepted and server is ready for client authentication.

Otherwise it starts with -ERR and server drops the connection or waits for client to drop the connection.

-ERR response can be caused by a number of reasons: you are not allowed to access the server (your IP is blacklisted, or not in whitelist), too many connections from your IP address, mailserver is down for maintenance, server software error, etc.

Session can't be established after that initial -ERR status response. You need to close the connection and try to connect again.

Maybe wait for a couple minutes before re-connecting if it's a server error. Or call server admin and ask to add your IP to whitelist, if it's an access issue.

We already have a variable to hold server responses, so let's use it.

To get initial status response add the following code right after `SetConnectionType();` call:

```
_response = Receive();
if (_response.ToUpper().StartsWith("-ERR"))
    throw new Exception(_response);
```

Retrieving and managing email with POP3 and C#

We call previously declared `Receive` method and load its result into `_response` variable.

If it's an error, then we throw an exception to invoke `catch` part of our connect block.

Since we are already connected at this point, it makes sense to introduce the code for disconnecting:

```
private void Quit()
{
    txtMessageCount.Text = "0";
    txtMailboxSize.Text = "0";
    lvwMessages.Items.Clear();

    if (_response.ToUpper().StartsWith("-ERR "))
        txtStatus.Text += "\r\n! " + _response.Substring(4).Trim();

    SetUI(State.Closing);

    try
    {
        if (_client.Connected)
        {
            SendCommand("QUIT");
            _client.Close();
        }
    }
    catch { }

    SetUI(State.Closed);
    _client = null;
    _command = "";
    _response = "";
}
```

Now that's a very thorough way to close a connection.

First, we reset the contents of mailbox controls.

Then, if we are closing the connection due to an error, status textbox gets updated with error message.

Set UI status to intermediate - check.

Issue **QUIT** command if client is still connected - check.

Just in case, explicitly close the client (even though it's likely to be closed by now) - check.

Set UI status to solid `Closed` - done.

Reset session level variables - done.

Wow.

There is one thing missing, though - we haven't defined `SendCommand()` method yet.

So here it is:

```
private bool SendCommand(string commandName)
{
    return SendCommand(commandName, commandName);
}

private bool SendCommand(string commandName, string commandText)
{
    _command = commandName;
    Send(commandText);

    _response = Receive();
    return (_response.ToUpper().StartsWith("+OK"));
}
```

Why do we need an overload? Well, in some cases command name and command text are the same (for example, STAT, RSET, QUIT). Sometimes we need to be more verbal when it comes to a command text (TOP vs TOP 1 20, RETR vs RETR 15, etc.)

Just a reminder, we are using command name to determine whether mailserver response is complete (switch in `IsComplete()` method).

11. Authentication (commands USER and PASS)

Now, after we implemented the framework for sending commands to POP3 server and reading its responses, we can proceed to authenticate to a mailbox of our choice.

For that we will need to provide server with mailbox username and password.

The following line goes into `btnConnect_Click` right after checking the server response:

```
Authenticate();
```

And here is the implementation:

```
private void Authenticate()
{
    SetUI(State.Authenticating);

    SendCommand("USER", "USER " + txtUsername.Text);
    if (SendCommand("PASS", "PASS " + txtPassword.Text))
        SetUI(State.Authenticated);
    else
        throw new Exception(_response);
}
```

Everything is so simple with the wrappers we created for communicating with mailserver and for managing GUI!

If authentication fails at any point (wrong username or password, or connectivity problem, or server error) `Authenticate()` method will close the session, disconnect from the server and raise an error in `btnConnect_Click` call.

Otherwise, we are connected to the server, POP3 session is established and we are ready to rock-n-roll!

Sorry, I meant to read and manage the mailbox content.

12. Retrieving mailbox stats (STAT command)

So far we have connected to mailserver, authenticated to a mailbox. The next logical step will be to retrieve mailbox statistics - its size and number of messages in it.

STAT command does just that and using it is very straightforward:

```
private void GetMailboxStats()
{
    txtMessageCount.Text = "0";
    txtMailboxSize.Text = "0";

    if (SendCommand("STAT"))
    {
        string s = _response.Substring(3).Trim();
        int n = s.IndexOf(" ");
        if (n > 0)
        {
            txtMessageCount.Text = s.Substring(0, n);
            txtMailboxSize.Text = s.Substring(n + 1);
        }
    }
}
```

Let's add `GetMailboxStats()` call to `btnConnect_Click()` method right after `Authenticate()`

13. Getting message list (LIST command)

We will use a response to **LIST** command to populate our message treeview with the list of available messages:

```
private void GetMessageList()
{
    lvwMessages.Items.Clear();

    if (!SendCommand("LIST"))
        return;

    string sList = _response.Substring(3).Trim();

    sList = sList.Replace("\r\n", "\n");
    string[] a;
    int n = 0;

    a = sList.Split('\n');
    for (int i = 0; i < a.Length; i++)
    {
        n = a[i].IndexOf(" ");
        if (n > 0)
        {
            ListViewItem li =
lvwMessages.Items.Add(a[i].Substring(0, n));
            li.SubItems.Add(a[i].Substring(n + 1));
        }
    }
}
```

And a corresponding call to `GetMessageList()` goes into `btnConnect_Click()` method right after `GetMailboxStats()`

14. Finalizing btnConnect_Click() method

As you may recall, we were planning to use **btnConnect** for both - connecting and disconnecting the session. It'll be done based on a button caption.

The complete and final code for `btnConnect_Click()` method is below. And, at least for this project, there isn't going to be any changes to it. Finito.

```
private void btnConnect_Click(object sender, EventArgs e)
{
    if (btnConnect.Text == "Connect")
    {
        SetUI(State.Connecting);
        try
        {
            _client = new TcpClient(txtServer.Text, Convert.ToInt32(txtPort.Text));
            SetUI(State.Connected);

            SetConnectionType();

            _response = Receive();
            if (_response.ToUpper().StartsWith("-ERR"))
                throw new Exception(_response);

            Authenticate();
            GetMailboxStats();
            GetMessageList();
        }
        catch (Exception ex)
        {
            txtStatus.Text += "\r\n! " + ex.Message;
```

```
            _response = "";
            Quit();
            return;
        }
    }
    else
        Quit();
}
```

One last finishing touch, before we move to dealing with messages, is adding a method to call when closing the form. Just a simple cleanup procedure:

```
private void frmSession_FormClosing(object sender, FormClosingEventArgs e)
{
    try {
        Quit();
    } catch { }
}
```

That'll prevent us from losing changes made during POP3 session if we accidentally close the form without clicking "Quit" button first.

15. Session reset (RSET command)

Command **RSET** restores the initial state of POP3 session - namely, it will undelete all messages deleted during the session.

We will execute it by clicking button **btnResetSession**.

Double-click on the button in design view for **frmSession**. It will create an event handler in form designer and a corresponding method in form code. Edit the method to look like this:

```
private void btnResetSession_Click(object sender, EventArgs e)
{
    SendCommand("RSET");
    GetMailboxStats();
    GetMessageList();
}
```

After resetting the session we are reloading the mailbox stats and its message list. And that's all for button **btnResetSession**.

Button **btnRefreshMsgList** simply refreshes the message list.
Double-click on it in design view and edit its method as follows:

```
private void btnRefreshMsgList_Click(object sender, EventArgs e)
{
    GetMessageList();
}
```

16. Deleting a message (DELE command)

Double-click on button **btnDeleteMessage** in **frmSession** design view. It will generate a method stub for button click.

Modify the method to issue **DELE** command and to remove a selected message from listview if command was successfully executed:

```
private void btnDeleteMessage_Click(object sender,
EventArgs e)
{
    if (lvwMessages.SelectedItems.Count == 0)
        return;

    ListViewItem selectedMessage =
lvwMessages.SelectedItems[0];
    if (SendCommand("DELE", "DELE " +
selectedMessage.Text))
    {
        selectedMessage.Remove();
    }
}
```

* Deleted messages can be restored during the session by issuing **RSET** command

17. Email message format.

Before we start retrieving messages, let's talk about message format.

Message headers.

Every message has headers - a bunch of information fields in a format `<header-name>:<header-value>`

Examples of a popular message headers are message subject, date when the message was sent, sender, recipient, etc.

Header may have multiple values. They are separate by semicolon `<header-name>:<header-value1>;<header-value2>;<header-value1>`

Header is terminated by new line characters (`<CR><LF>`), but there is a catch.

For backward compatibility with legacy implementations, standards, defining the message format, recommend a single line not to exceed 78 characters.

If total length of a header exceeds the limit, the header needs to be "folded" by inserting a combination of `<CR><LF><WS>` characters (where `<WS>` is any whitespace character - TAB or SPACE).

When parsing email headers they need to be "unfolded" - assembled back in a single line by removing `<CR><LF><WS>` separators.

Message body.

Header section is optionally followed by message body.
Note the "optionally" part - it's perfectly fine, though rare, for a message to contain only headers.

Header section and message body are separated by an empty line.

In a most basic case, message body is just a bunch of ASCII characters - plain text.

Encoding.

Of course, nothing is basic in email world - what about non-ASCII characters and binary attachments?

This is handled by message encoding - replacing non-ASCII characters with a combination of ASCII characters according to a specified algorithm.

The most popular encoding schemes are **Base64** and **Quoted-Printable**.

Content-Transfer-Encoding header in headers section indicates that message is encoded and needs to be decoded before reading. For example:
```
Content-Transfer-Encoding: quoted-printable
```

Headers can be encoded as well. Message subjects written in foreign languages, sender or recipient names may contain non-ASCII characters.

Encoded header embeds information about encoding scheme and underlying character set. For example:
```
From: =?iso-8859-1?B?<encoded-string>?=
```

"=?" and "?=" sequences delimit encoded part of the header, "iso-8859-1" means that header was originally written in iso-8859-1 charset and should be decoded using it.

"B" means that Base64 algorithm was used to encode the string ("P" stands for quoted-printable).

Body parts.

I am not talking about anatomy. A body of internet message may contain various parts: plain-text part for reading in basic email clients, HTML part for reading in clients supporting HTML, attachments and embedded images.

Parts are separated by **boundaries** - pre-defined lines of characters.

Parts can be nested like Matryoshka dolls - inside each other. Each level of parts has its own boundaries.

Message part format mimics a message format - it has a header section and a part body separated by an empty line.

Format of a message part is defined in **Content-Type** header.

For example, message having both plain-text and HTML parts will have something like this in its header section:

```
Content-Type: multipart/alternative;
    boundary="----=_NextPart_000_0006_01C6C75A.8F65DF00"
```

its plain-text part will start with the following:

```
------=_NextPart_000_0006_01C6C75A.8F65DF00
Content-Type: text/plain;
    charset="us-ascii"
Content-Transfer-Encoding: 7bit
```

and HTML part will be preceded by

```
------=_NextPart_000_0006_01C6C75A.8F65DF00
Content-Type: text/html;
    charset="us-ascii"
Content-Transfer-Encoding: quoted-printable
```

Content-Type: `multipart/mixed`; indicates that message has binary attachments.

18. Retrieving messages (RETR and TOP commands)

TOP is not a mandatory POP3 command - meaning some mailserver implementations may not support it. But most of them do. The most popular at least.

TOP command allows you to "peek" into a message without retrieving its full content. This is helpful when you just want to see a subject of a potentially large message.

The full syntax for TOP command is:
`TOP <number-of-message> <number-of-lines>`

TOP always retrieves message headers and first few lines of its body (specified in `<number-of-lines>` parameter). If `<number-of-lines>` is 0 mailserver will return only message headers.

RETR retrieves an entire message.

We will use both commands when clicking on buttons **btnViewMessage** and **btnViewHeaders**

```
private void btnViewMessage_Click(object sender,
EventArgs e)
{
    ViewMessage("RETR");
}
```

Retrieving and managing email with POP3 and C#

```
private void btnViewHeaders_Click(object sender,
EventArgs e)
{
    ViewMessage("TOP");
}
```

Let's put together `ViewMessage()` method.

As you can see it's used by both buttons. The difference is only in POP3 command syntax and, of course, in the result:

```
private void ViewMessage(string command)
{
    if (lvwMessages.SelectedItems.Count == 0)
        return;

    ListViewItem selectedMessage =
lvwMessages.SelectedItems[0];
    string commandText = "";
    switch (command)
    {
        case "TOP":
            commandText = "TOP " + selectedMessage.Text + " 0";
            break;
        case "RETR":
            commandText = "RETR " + selectedMessage.Text;
            break;
    }

    if (SendCommand(command, commandText))
    {
        string messageSource = _response;
        messageSource =
messageSource.Substring(messageSource.IndexOf("\r\n") + 2);
//remove status string
        messageSource = messageSource.Substring(0,
messageSource.Length - "\r\n.\r\n".Length); //remove
response terminator

        frmMessage frm = new frmMessage();
        frm.messageID = selectedMessage.Text;
        frm.messageSource = messageSource;
        frm.ShowDialog();
    }
}
```

And that completes the code for **frmSession**. Message parsing and rendering will be done in **frmMessage**.

19. frmMessage

Add a new form to your project, name it **frmMessage**. Add a TreeView **tvw** and a button **btnSave** to the form.

The form should look like this:

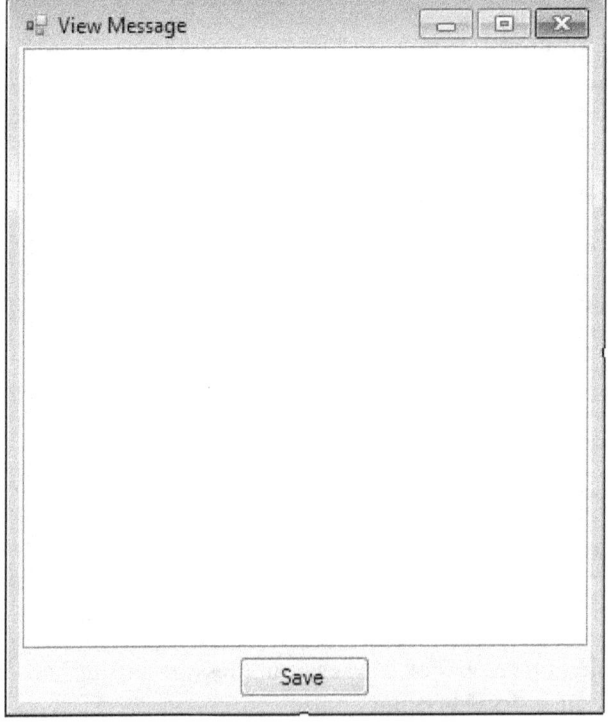

Make sure its code has the following declarations:

```
using System;
using System.IO;
using System.Windows.Forms;
```

Add public variables to hold message ID and source when called from **frmSession**:

```
public string messageID = "";
public string messageSource = "";
```

Double-click on the form and enter the following code to its Load event method:

```
private void frmMessage_Load(object sender, System.EventArgs e)
{
    tvw.Nodes.Clear();
    TreeNode ndPart = tvw.Nodes.Add("message");
    ParsePart(messageSource, ndPart);
}
```

That's it, we are done.

Kidding, the fun has just started!

20. ParsePart() method

Why are we calling `ParsePart()` method if we need to parse a message?

Remember Matryoshka effect! Message is just a top level part containing parts containing parts.

We will re-use `ParsePart()` method for each one of them recursively.

As you can see from the code below, `ParsePart()` does the following:
- sets all line breaks to UNIX style (easier to handle)
- removes all mailserver status junk (leading +OK, trailing ".")
- separates header from body
- "unfolds" headers
- calls `LoadHeaders()` method

```
private void ParsePart(string partSource, TreeNode ndPart)
{
    string part = partSource.Replace("\r\n", "\n"); //set all line breaks to UNIX style
    string partHeader = "";
    string partBody = "";

    part = part.Substring(part.IndexOf("\n") + 1); //remove status string (+OK ...)
    int n = part.IndexOf("\n.\n");
    if (n > 0)
        part = part.Substring(0, n); //remove message terminator (.)
```

```
        n = part.IndexOf("\n\n"); //divider between headers and
body
        if (n > 0)
        {
            partHeader = part.Substring(0, n);
            partBody = part.Substring(n + 2);
        }
        else
            partHeader = part;

        partHeader = partHeader.Replace("\n ", " "); //unfold
headers
        partHeader = partHeader.Replace("\n\t", " "); //unfold
headers
        partHeader = partHeader.Replace("\t", ""); //remove
tabs

        LoadHeaders(partHeader, partBody, ndPart);
}
```

21. LoadHeaders() method

In this method we loop through the collection of message headers and display them in **frmMessage** treeview hierarchically.

Since content-related headers will be used later when parsing part body, we treat them with extra attention and load into variables (`contentType`, `contentTransferEncoding` and `partBoundary`).

Also, all encoded headers are automatically decoded using `DecodeString()` method.

Finally, if there is a part body, it's processed in `LoadBody()` call.

```
private void LoadHeaders(string partHeader, string
partBody, TreeNode ndPart)
{
    string contentType = "";
    string contentTransferEncoding = "";
    string partBoundary = "";

    TreeNode ndHeaders = ndPart.Nodes.Add("headers");
    TreeNode ndHeader;
    string headerName = "";
    string[] headerValues;
    string headerValue = "";
    string[] headers = partHeader.Split('\n');
    int n = 0;

    for (int i = 0; i < headers.Length; i++)
    {
        n = headers[i].IndexOf(":");
        if (n > 1)
        {
            headerName = headers[i].Substring(0, n).Trim();
```

```csharp
            headerValues = headers[i].Substring(n + 1).Trim().Split(';');

            ndHeader = ndHeaders.Nodes.Add(headerName);
            foreach (string s in headerValues)
                ndHeader.Nodes.Add(DecodeString(s.Trim()));

            if (headerName.ToLower() == "content-type")
            {
                foreach (string s in headerValues)
                {
                    headerValue = s.Trim();
                    if (headerValue.IndexOf("=") < 0)
                        contentType = headerValue;
                    if (headerValue.ToLower().IndexOf("boundary=") == 0)
                        partBoundary = headerValue.Substring(headerValue.IndexOf("=") + 1).Replace("\"", "").Trim();
                }
            }
            if (headerName.ToLower() == "content-transfer-encoding")
            {
                foreach (string s in headerValues)
                {
                    headerValue = s.Trim();
                    if (headerValue != "")
                        contentTransferEncoding = headerValue.ToLower();
                }
            }
        }
    }
    if (ndHeaders.Nodes.Count == 0)
        ndHeaders.Remove();

    if (partBody != "")
    {
        TreeNode ndBody = ndPart.Nodes.Add("body");
        LoadBody(partBody, ndBody, contentType, contentTransferEncoding, partBoundary);
        ndBody.Expand();
    }

    if (ndPart.Nodes.Count == 0)
        ndPart.Remove();
    else
        ndPart.Expand();
}
```

22. DecodeString() method

This method detects whether header is encoded (based on leading "=?" and trailing "?=" sequences).

If it's the case - extracts the encoding type (Base64 or QuotedPrintableDecode) and calls a corresponding method to decode header value.

```
private string DecodeString(string s)
{
    if (s.StartsWith("=?") && s.EndsWith("?=")) //encoded
    {
        string encType = "";
        string encHeader = "";
        int encStart = 0;

        encStart = s.IndexOf("?B?");
        if (encStart > 0)
        {
            encType = "B";
            encHeader = s.Substring(0, encStart + 3);
        }
        else
        {
            encStart = s.IndexOf("?Q?");
            if (encStart > 0)
            {
                encType = "Q";
                encHeader = s.Substring(0, encStart + 3);
            }
        }
```

```
            if (encStart > 0)
            {
                s = s.Replace("?= ", "?="); //remove space between string parts
                s = s.Replace("?=" + encHeader, ""); //join string parts
                s = s.Replace(encHeader, ""); //remove leading header
                if (s.EndsWith("?="))
                    s = s.Substring(0, s.Length - 2); //remove trailing ?=

                switch (encType)
                {
                    case "B": //Base64
                        s = Base64Decode(s);
                        break;
                    case "Q": //Quoted-Printable
                        s = QuotedPrintableDecode(s);
                        break;
                }
            }
        }
        return s;
    }
```

23. Decoding functions (Base64 and Quoted-Printable)

.NET has built-in functions to deal with Base64 and we will gladly use them:

```
private string Base64Decode(string sourceString)
{
    return
Convert.FromBase64String(sourceString).ToString();
}
```

No such luck when it comes to quoted-printable.
Fortunately, decoding algorithm is not complicated:

```
private string QuotedPrintableDecode(string sourceString)
{
    sourceString = sourceString.Replace("=\n", "");
//unfold Q-wrapping

    string _output = "";
    string _hex = "";//holds hexadecimal value
    int _dec = 0;//holds ASCII value

    for (int i = 0; i < sourceString.Length; i++)
    {
        switch (sourceString[i])
        {
            case '=': //ASCII non-character =hh
                _hex = sourceString[i + 1].ToString() +
sourceString[i + 2].ToString();
```

```
                    _dec = Convert.ToInt32(_hex, 16);
                    _output = _output + (char)_dec;
                    i = i + 2;
                    break;
                default: //ASCII character
                    _output = _output + sourceString[i];
                    break;
            }
        }
        return _output;
    }
```

24. LoadBody() method

This method extracts body part, decodes it if necessary, loads to treeview and calls `ParsePart()` method if underlying parts are detected (recursion! yes!!)

```
private void LoadBody(string partBody, TreeNode ndBody,
string contentType, string contentTransferEncoding, string
partBoundary)
{
    ndBody.Parent.Text = contentType;
    if (contentType.StartsWith("multipart"))
    {
        string[] bodyParts = partBody.Split(new string[] {
partBoundary }, StringSplitOptions.None);
        foreach (string bodyPart in bodyParts)
        {
            if (bodyPart != "==")
            {
                TreeNode ndBodyPart =
ndBody.Nodes.Add(contentType);
                ParsePart(bodyPart, ndBodyPart);
            }
        }
    }
    else
    {
        if ((contentType == "text/html") || (contentType ==
"text/plain"))
        {
            ndBody.Nodes.Add(DecodePartBody(partBody,
contentTransferEncoding));
        }
        else
```

```
            {
                ndBody.Nodes.Add(partBody);
            }
    }
}
```

```
private string DecodePartBody(string partBody, string contentTransferEncoding)
{
    string decodedPartBody = "";
    switch (contentTransferEncoding)
    {
        case "quoted-printable":
            decodedPartBody = QuotedPrintableDecode(partBody);
            break;
        case "base64":
            decodedPartBody = Base64Decode(partBody);
            break;
        default:
            decodedPartBody = partBody;
            break;
    }
    return decodedPartBody;
}
```

25. Saving the message

We are pretty much done with **frmMessage**.

The last finishing touch - adding an ability to save the loaded message.

Double-click on button **btnSave** in form design view, add the following code to the generated method:

```
private void btnSave_Click(object sender, EventArgs e)
{
    dlgFolder.ShowDialog();
    string path = dlgFolder.SelectedPath;

    string filename = path + "\\" + messageID.ToString() + ".eml";
    StreamWriter sw = new StreamWriter(filename);
    sw.Write(messageSource);
    sw.Close();
    MessageBox.Show("message saved");
}
```

26. Running the application

If you paid attention to details, the application should compile and run on the first start.

Go on - run it, enter your mailserver credentials and click "Connect". You should see something like this:

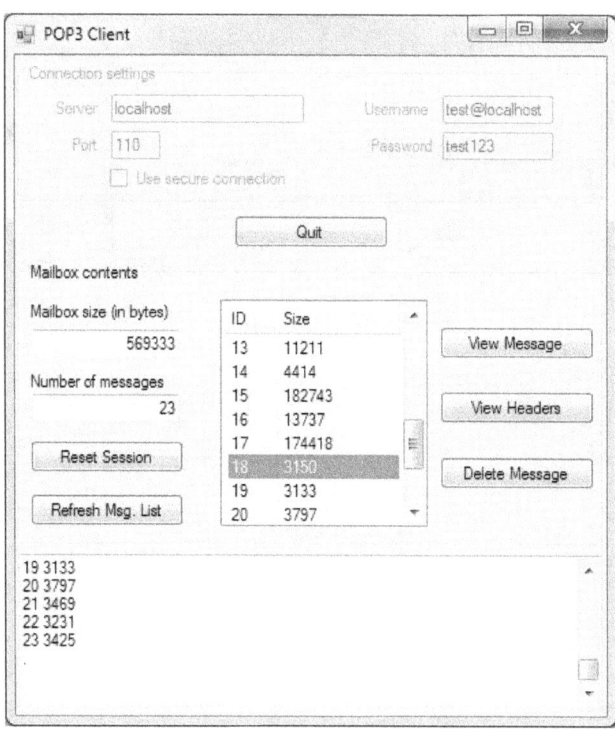

I am going to pick my favorite message number 18 and click "View Message".

Here it is in all its parsed beauty:

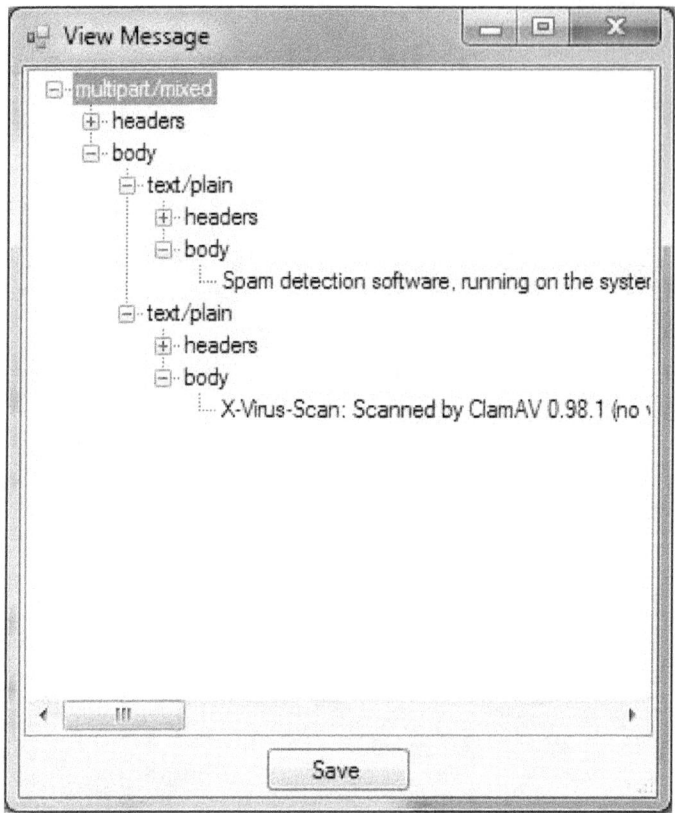

Move mouse over body node in treeview to see its content

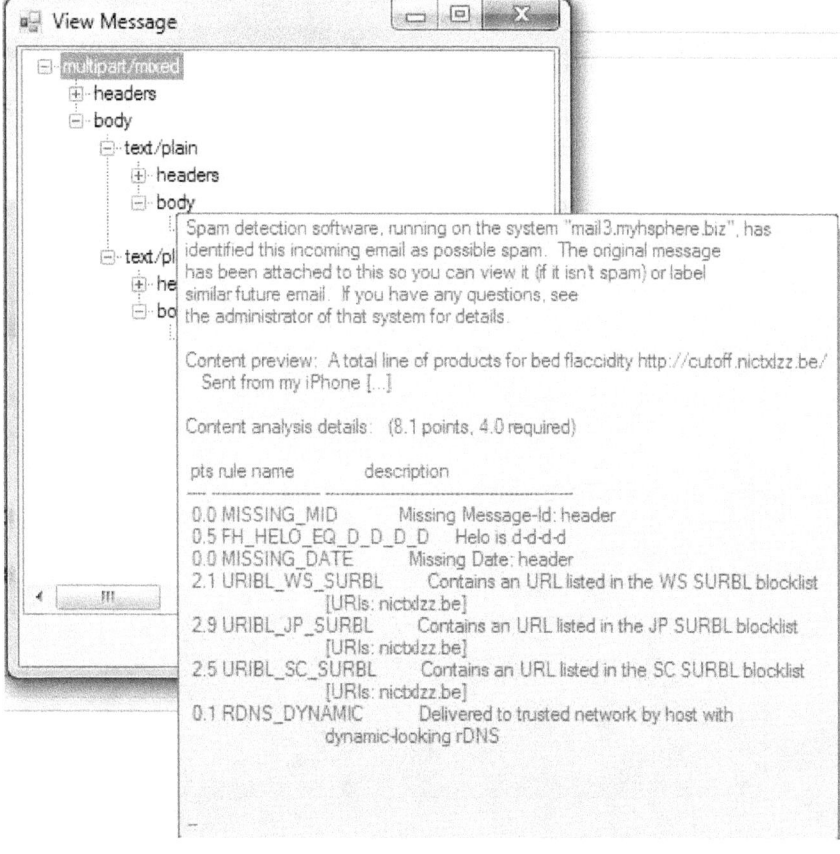

Expand headers

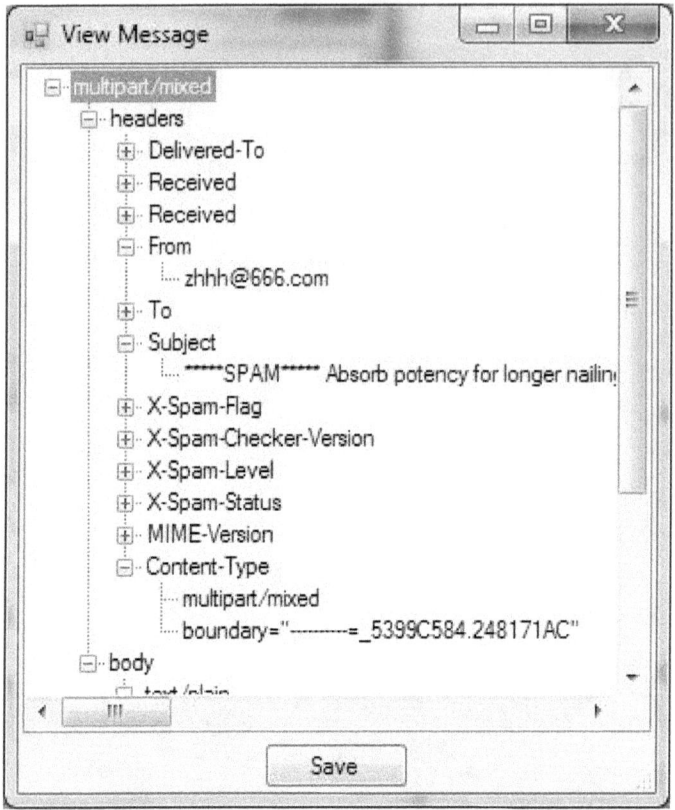

Save the message and view it in your favorite app (Notepad, of course)

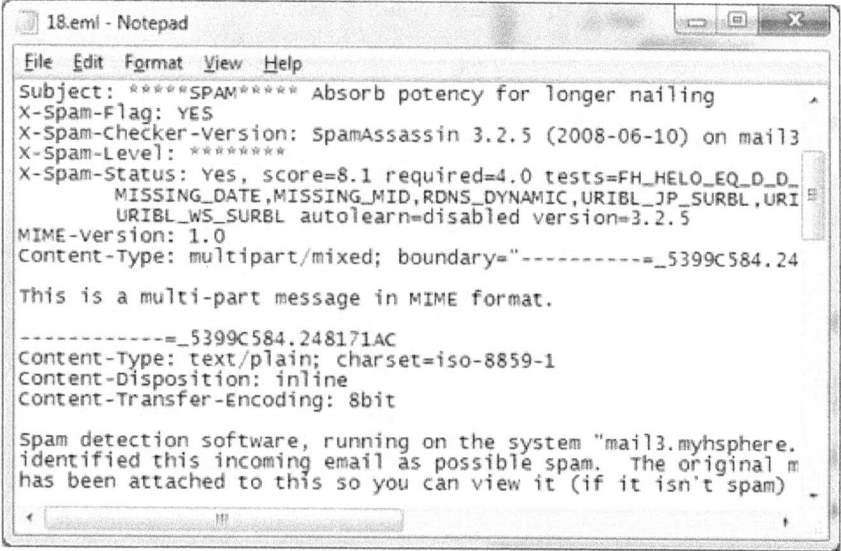

Delete the message, reset the session, refresh mailbox stats - possibilities are endless!

And that concludes our foray into the wonderful world of POP3.

Links and references

Post Office Protocol - Version 3
http://tools.ietf.org/html/rfc1939

Internet Message Format
http://tools.ietf.org/html/rfc5322

OstroSoft POP3 Component
http://www.ostrosoft.com/ospop3.aspx

Wikipedia about Post Office Protocol
http://en.wikipedia.org/wiki/Post_Office_Protocol

PuTTY (secure telnet client)
http://www.chiark.greenend.org.uk/~sgtatham/putty/download.html

Multipurpose Internet Mail Extensions (MIME)
http://tools.ietf.org/html/rfc2045
http://tools.ietf.org/html/rfc2046
http://tools.ietf.org/html/rfc2047
http://tools.ietf.org/html/rfc2049
http://tools.ietf.org/html/rfc2231
http://tools.ietf.org/html/rfc3676
http://tools.ietf.org/html/rfc3798
http://tools.ietf.org/html/rfc4289
http://tools.ietf.org/html/rfc5147
http://tools.ietf.org/html/rfc6532
http://tools.ietf.org/html/rfc6533
http://tools.ietf.org/html/rfc6657

Other books written by me

Reading Excel Data with C# and Open XML: Basics and implementation
http://www.amazon.com/dp/B00IK9DJ74

www.ingramcontent.com/pod-product-compliance
Lightning Source LLC
Chambersburg PA
CBHW071809170526
45167CB00003B/1235